# Reading for Central Message and Details in Literature

Grade 3

## Table of Contents



**Free Video Tutorial**

Use this QR code to launch a short video that provides instruction for skills featured in this book. To access the video from your smartphone or tablet:

- Download a free QR code scanner from your device's app store.
- Launch the scanning app on your device.
- Scan the code to visit the web page for this book.
- Find the video under the Resources tab.

This *Spectrum Focus* video is also available at:
- http://www.carsondellosa.com/704902
- www.youtube.com/user/CarsonDellosaPub


Spectrum®
An imprint of Carson-Dellosa Publishing LLC
P.O. Box 35665
Greensboro, NC 27425





ISBN 978-1-4838-2419-2

02-226157784

# Focus On Reading for Central Message and Details

Thinking about the key ideas and details of stories enhances our enjoyment and understanding of literature. Readers of fiction can use many strategies to increase comprehension. These include asking and answering questions, finding the central message conveyed through a story's details, and describing the feelings and actions of characters. For each of these skills, *Reading for Central Message and Details in Literature* provides step-by-step teaching, explanations, and practice. Close reading of short literary passages is followed by text-based comprehension questions that build critical-thinking skills.

Read this text closely. It will be used to illustrate the topics that follow.

**Rainbow Crow: A Lenape Tale**

1 Long ago, before there was man, the crow was the most exquisite bird in the world. His wings were made of rainbow feathers, and his voice was the sweetest ever heard.

2 Then one day, snow came to the forest for the first time ever. The animals thought little of it at first, but soon Mouse was completely buried. They had to stop the snow before it covered everyone. Rainbow Crow offered to fly to the Great Sky Spirit and ask him to stop the snow.

3 Rainbow Crow flew high toward the spirits for three days. At last, he reached the Great Sky Spirit and asked him to stop the snow. The Great One said that he could not grant the request because the snow had its own spirit. He offered the gift of fire to warm the earth instead. He gave the bird a flaming stick to carry in his mouth back to the forest.

4 Rainbow Crow flew quickly toward Earth. On the first day, sparks from the flame burned his tail feathers, but he bravely flew on. The next day, he noticed his wing feathers were covered with black soot. On the third day, Rainbow Crow could barely breathe from the fire burning his throat, but he reached the woods just in time. His friends were completely buried now, so Rainbow Crow used the flame to melt the snow.

5 Crow looked at himself. He was no longer beautiful, and his voice had become cracked and raspy. Crow began to cry. The Great

Sky Spirit appeared to him. He explained that one day man would come to Earth and hunt animals. He gave Crow the gift of freedom. "Man will not want your meat or your plain black feathers," he said. "But, you will always know your true beauty. Look closely at your feathers, for you will see all the colors of the rainbow reflecting in them." Crow returned to his friends in the forest, feeling proud, brave, and beautiful.

## Asking Questions About a Text

When you read a story or poem, it is normal to have many questions. Texts may include new words, unfamiliar situations, and characters whose lives are different from yours. Asking questions about all these things will help you understand what you read. It is a good idea to ask questions before you read, while you are reading, and after you read. When you read a story or poem, ask questions like the ones shown below. They begin with these question words: *Who? What? Where? When? Why? How?*

**Rainbow Crow: A Lenape Tale**

1 Long ago, before there was man, the crow was the most exquisite bird in the world. His wings were made of rainbow feathers, and his voice was the sweetest ever heard.

2 Then one day, snow came to the forest for the first time ever. The animals thought little of it at first, but soon Mouse was completely buried. They had to stop the snow before it covered everyone. Rainbow Crow offered to fly to the Great Sky Spirit and ask him to stop the snow.

When does this story take place?

What does this word mean?

How does a crow's voice usually sound?

Why was snow new for the animals?

Where was Mouse?

Who is this?

# Focus On Reading for Central Message and Details

## Answering Questions About a Text

Most questions about stories can be answered by looking closely at what the text says. For example, if you don't understand the meaning of a word, search the surrounding sentences for context clues. If you come to a part you don't understand, reread it carefully. Go back to a part you understood well and read again from there. As they read, good readers ask and answer many questions.

Sometimes, you will be asked to answer questions to show someone else that you understand a text. Readers may be asked to answer these types of questions during a class discussion, for homework, or on a test.

Many questions can be answered by finding the place in the text that contains the correct information. Sometimes, you will need to combine information found in several different places in the story. Look at these examples.

3 Rainbow Crow flew high toward the spirits for three days. At last, he reached the Great Sky Spirit and asked him to stop the snow. The Great One said that he could not grant the request because the snow had its own spirit. He offered the gift of fire to warm the earth instead. He gave the bird a flaming stick to carry in his mouth back to the forest.

How long did it take Rainbow Crow to reach the Great Sky Spirit? He had to fly for three days to get there.

Why did the Great One give Rainbow Crow fire? He gave Rainbow Crow fire to warm the snowy earth.

Give two names for the spirit that Rainbow Crow goes to see. Two names for the spirit are Great Sky Spirit and the Great One.

How did the Great Sky Spirit give Rainbow Crow the gift of fire? He gave the bird a flaming stick to carry.

## Determining the Central Message, Lesson, or Moral

Most stories teach a lesson, make a point, or have a strong message. This *central message* is the most important idea that the author of a story wants readers to understand and remember. The central message is often in the form of a lesson.

To find the central message of a story, identify the key events. If a key event leads to a clear outcome, then the author is sending a message. Think of a central message as a life lesson. Imagine that you left your bike out in the rain. Later, when you wanted to ride it, the chain was rusted out. Because one key event (leaving your bike out) caused another key event (the chain's rusting), you might learn the lesson *Take care of your things.* The same is true for a central message.

- *Fables* are traditional stories with animal characters that act and talk like people. The central message in a fable is called a *moral* (a good way of thinking or acting). In the fable "The Tortoise and the Hare," the speedy hare is so certain she will win the race that she takes a nap. Meanwhile, the slow tortoise passes her by and wins. The moral is *Slow and steady wins the race.*
- *Folktales* are traditional stories passed down from one generation to the next. A folktale reflects the customs of the people who tell it and teaches a lesson that is important to that culture. In the folktale "Stone Soup," some hungry soldiers enter a village. No one offers to share food with them, so the tricksters boil rocks. One by one, the villagers come to see the soup and add a vegetable to the pot. Soon, there is tasty soup for all. The lesson is *When people share, there is enough for all.*
- *Myths* are stories that explain how something came to be or why something is. A myth is told by people who share a culture and is often sacred to those people. "Rainbow Crow," on page 2, is a myth from the Native American Lenape people. It explains why crows are black and why people do not hunt them. Like other stories, myths have strong messages. In "Rainbow Crow," Crow is strong, brave, and helpful, even though his appearance has turned ugly. The central message of "Rainbow Crow" is *Know your true beauty.*

## Finding Details that Support the Central Message, Lesson, or Moral

Details are the parts of a story that add up to the main message or lesson. Details can be problems or situations described in a story, events that happen, the thoughts and feelings of characters, or choices that characters make. All the details in a story come together to show the central message in a way that readers will enjoy, understand, and remember.

# Focus On Reading for Central Message and Details

The lesson of "Rainbow Crow: A Lenape Tale" from page 2 is "Know your true beauty." Look at details from the story shown below. Read the explanation about how each detail supports the story's message.

1 Long ago, before there was man, the crow was the most exquisite bird in the world. His wings were made of rainbow feathers, and his voice was the sweetest ever heard.

This detail shows that Crow was once beautiful on the outside. So, by the end of the story, he knows the difference between this type of beauty and "true beauty."

4 Rainbow Crow flew quickly toward Earth. On the first day, sparks from the flame burned his tail feathers, but he bravely flew on. The next day, he noticed his wing feathers were covered with black soot. On the third day, Rainbow Crow could barely breathe from the fire burning his throat, but he reached the woods just in time. His friends were completely buried now, so Rainbow Crow used the flame to melt the snow.

These details show how Crow's feathers became black and how his throat got burnt. His body was damaged because he was trying to help his friends. At the end of the story, he understands that "true beauty" comes from doing good, not from looking good.

He explained that one day man would come to Earth and hunt animals. He gave Crow the gift of freedom. "Man will not want your meat or your plain black feathers," he said. "But, you will always know your true beauty. Look closely at your feathers, for you will see all the colors of the rainbow reflecting in them." Crow returned to his friends in the forest, feeling proud, brave, and beautiful.

This detail tells what Rainbow Crow gains at the end of the story. Crow gets freedom from being hunted and also the freedom of knowing that he is beautiful on the inside no matter how he appears on the outside.

This detail tells how Rainbow Crow feels after he knows his true beauty.

# **Focus On** Reading for Central Message and Details

## Describing Characters

Characters are the most fascinating part of many stories. Characters can be people, animals, space aliens, or something else. They can bake pies, dance in the rain, sail on purple seas, and do anything else you can imagine. A character's thoughts, feelings, attitudes, and actions are very important to the way a story unfolds. Often, decisions that characters make determine what happens in a story. There are many ways to describe characters. Look at these examples.

*Traits*

Characters can be described by physical traits such as height, weight, hair color, style of moving, and tone of voice. They can also be described by personality traits such as shyness, sense of humor, creativity, and kindness. Look closely at the text to find out what traits a character has. Don't assume that a character is like someone you know. Instead, rely on the evidence the author gives in the text.

The author of "Rainbow Crow" tells readers that Crow has beautiful rainbow-colored feathers and a sweet voice (at the beginning of the story), and plain black feathers and a raspy voice (at the end of the story). Evidence from the text also shows that Crow is brave (because he volunteers to visit the Great Sky Spirit) and strong (because he flies for three days carrying a flaming stick).

*Feelings and Motivations*

In many stories, the author describes a character's thoughts and feelings. In "Rainbow Crow," Crow feels sad when he sees his changed appearance. By reading a text closely, readers can determine a character's *motivations*, or desires and wishes. Crow volunteers to fly to the Great Sky Spirit. He faces danger by flying with a flaming stick. He uses fire to melt the snow. This evidence shows that Crow is very motivated to help his friends and the earth.

*Actions*

Readers learn a lot about a character through his or her actions. The decisions that characters make and the actions they take determine what happens in a story and what kind of ending the story has. In "Rainbow Crow," Crow is the animal who offers to fly to the Great Sky Spirit. This brave act sets off a chain of events. Because he makes the journey, he must carry the flame to save Earth. The flame changes his appearance. Crow's new appearance causes his life to change forever. All these story events are the result of Crow's decision.

NAME ______________________

# Literature Asking Questions

Read the passage. Use it to answer the questions on pages 9 and 10.

## Nighttime Visitors

1 "Come on, Jackson," called Mr. Wylon. "Time for bed."

2 "One more minute, Dad," pleaded Jackson from his perch by the window. "If I walk away, I'm going to miss something."

3 Mr. Wylon smiled. "It's past your bedtime. Let's get a move on!"

4 Jackson dragged himself away from the window and headed upstairs. He had been feeding a stray cat for over a month. Last week, Jackson's friend Akito had adopted the cat, so it had stopped coming for meals, but a nighttime visitor was still visiting Jackson's porch. He had forgotten to bring in the bowl of cat food. It was empty this morning and turned on its side. Jackson wondered what was eating the food if it wasn't the cat. What else was out there?

5 Jackson brushed his teeth half-heartedly. His mind was elsewhere. He kept thinking about everything that went on in his yard while he slept. Did owls hunt for mice under the oak tree? Did raccoons look for scraps of food he had dropped?

6 "I have an idea," said Mr. Wylon, as he tucked Jackson in. "We'll put an old white sheet out in the yard. We'll put some food, like granola, in the center. Then, we'll spray water on the ground around it. What do you think will happen?"

7 Jackson sat straight up in bed. "That's a great idea, Dad!" he exclaimed. "Night animals will come to check out the food, and they'll leave their footprints from the wet ground on the sheet."

8 "That's the idea," nodded Mr. Wylon.

9 Jackson whooped and jumped out of bed. "You get the sheet, Dad. I'll get the granola and some chopped-up apple pieces and meet you outside."

10 It took Jackson and his father only a few minutes to set everything up, but it took Jackson a long time to fall asleep. When he woke up in the morning, he raced downstairs. Mr. Wylon was already drinking coffee and checking e-mails. "I did not go look at the sheet without you," he said right away.

11 Together, Jackson and his dad went outside. A variety of footprints dotted the sheet. Jackson could identify deer and raccoon prints, as well as some possible dog prints. "Can we take some photos so we can identify the rest?" he asked. "Then, I want to wash the sheet so we can try again tonight!"

NAME ______________________

## Guided Practice Asking Questions

**1.** What questions can you ask about the beginning of the story to understand what is happening?

Sometimes, just asking a question will lead you to the answer. Asking specific questions about the text helps you figure out what is happening in a story. The question words *Who, What, Where, When, Why,* and *How* help you focus on important information in a story. When you ask a question, be sure to write it as a complete sentence.

In the beginning of "Nighttime Visitors," we meet the main characters. Reread paragraphs 1 through 3. Ask a "Who" question and a "What" question that focus on Jackson or Mr. Wylon.

Who ______________________________________________?

What ______________________________________________?

**2.** In paragraph 4, we are introduced to the mystery of the cat-food bowl. Reread the paragraph. What are three questions you could ask to make sure you understand the facts? Use the question words *What, When* (or *How long*), or *Where.*

______________________________________________

______________________________________________

______________________________________________

**3.** What questions can you ask about the beginning of the story to deepen your understanding?

Asking specific questions helps you get even closer to understanding what a story is all about. To gain a deeper understanding of the story, you will need to understand the "How" and "Why" of the story's main events.

Now that you have asked about the facts in paragraph 4, ask a "How" question and a "Why" question about the same paragraph.

______________________________________________

______________________________________________

NAME ____________________

## Independent Practice Asking Questions

1. If you knew something was eating the pet food you left outside during the night, what would you think? What questions would you ask?

___________________________________________

___________________________________________

2. Reread paragraph 5 below. Write a question about the underlined sentence.

> 5 Jackson brushed his teeth half-heartedly. His mind was elsewhere. He kept thinking about everything that went on in his yard while he slept. Did owls hunt for mice under the oak tree? Did raccoons look for scraps of food he had dropped?

___________________________________________

3. Imagine you're reading "Nighttime Visitors" to a younger child. You stop after paragraph 6 and ask, "What do you think will happen?" To help the child answer, what specific questions could you ask about the two steps in Mr. Wylon's plan?

___________________________________________

___________________________________________

4. Reread paragraph 9 and pay attention to the word *whooped.* Avoiding the question "What does *whooped* mean?" what could you ask to figure out the meaning?

___________________________________________

5. Underline something in the story that you would like to know more about. Then, ask a question about it.

___________________________________________

6. What other questions did the text leave unanswered for you?

___________________________________________

___________________________________________

NAME ______________________________

# Literature Answering Questions

Read the passage. Use it to answer the questions on pages 12 and 13.

## Demeter and Persephone

1 In Greek mythology, Demeter was the goddess of the earth and the harvest. She caused the crops to grow. She cared for the land and the life it gave to humans. More than anything, Demeter loved her daughter Persephone. Persephone helped her mother watch over and tend to seedlings and plants.

2 One day, Persephone was walking in a lovely field. She had stopped to gather some beautiful flowers. All of a sudden, a hole in the ground opened up before her. To her alarm, a chariot emerged from the earth. Persephone was seized by Hades, god of the underworld, who had taken her to be his queen.

3 Demeter was filled with sadness when she could not find her daughter. She searched everywhere in vain. In her grief, she could not sleep or eat. All she could do was search for her beloved Persephone. After some time, the sun took pity on Demeter. The sun told her that Hades had asked Zeus if he could take Persephone as his wife, and Zeus had agreed.

4 Demeter was very angry with her brother Zeus. She went into mourning for her daughter. As a result, she paid no attention to the land. Crops withered and died. Seeds were planted but did not come up. Nothing would grow. Zeus saw that something must be done. He knew that the people would starve if Demeter did not tend the earth as she had always done.

5 Zeus sent Hermes, a messenger, to the underworld. He told Hermes that he must bring back Persephone. Hermes went to the underworld to fetch her as he had been told. In her time with Hades, Persephone had eaten four seeds of a pomegranate fruit. It wasn't much, but because Persephone had eaten the food of the underworld, she had to stay there for four months of each year—one month for each pomegranate seed.

6 Persephone was allowed to return to the upper world for eight months of the year. In that time, the world was made fresh and new. Demeter again tended the land lovingly. Flowers and crops burst forth from the ground. But when it was time for Persephone to return to the underworld each year, a change came about. Demeter was again in mourning for her daughter. Plants and flowers died, and the world became cold, dark, and dreary. This is how, the Greeks believed, the seasons came about.

NAME ______________________________

## Guided Practice Answering Questions

**1.** What was Demeter's job as goddess of the earth and the harvest?

To answer this question, begin by skimming the first paragraph for the word *goddess*. You will find the line, "Demeter was the goddess of the earth and the harvest." Read on from there to find your answer. Then, circle the correct answer below.

Demeter's job was to

**A.** gather flowers.
**B.** harvest the crops.
**C.** give life to humans.
**D.** take care of the land.

Often, responses for a multiple choice question will be paraphrased. In other words, the exact words from the text may not be found in the answer choices. That means you have to make sure you understand both the information you read in the story and the words provided in the answer choices. Always choose the very best answer.

**2.** Who did Demeter love more than anything?

Answering this question is important for understanding the story as a whole. If you do not already know the answer, review paragraph 1 again. Then, fill in the blank below.

Demeter loved ____________________ more than anything.

**3.** Reread paragraph 2. How did Persephone feel when Hades's chariot came up from a hole in the earth?

To answer this question, you need to understand what "to her alarm" means. Consider what you know about alarms. For example, how do people feel when a fire alarm goes off? You might also think about how you yourself would feel if you watched a chariot spring up from the earth.

Which of these words best describes how Persephone felt at that moment?

**A.** afraid
**B.** awake
**C.** embarrassed
**D.** peaceful

NAME ______________________________

## Independent Practice Answering Questions

1. When she could not find her daughter, Demeter was filled with sadness. Which words from the text show how sad she was?

   **A.** She could not sleep or eat.

   **B.** The sun took pity on Demeter.

   **C.** She searched everywhere in vain.

   **D.** Demeter was very angry with her brother Zeus.

2. Why did Demeter stop paying attention to the land and its crops? Use evidence from the text to support your answer.

   ______________________________________________

   ______________________________________________

3. Reread paragraph 4 below. Underline the text that explains why Zeus decides to send Hermes to the underworld.

   4 Demeter was very angry with her brother Zeus. She went into mourning for her daughter. As a result, she paid no attention to the land. Crops withered and died. Seeds were planted but did not come up. Nothing would grow. Zeus saw that something must be done. He knew that the people would starve if Demeter did not tend the earth as she had always done.

4. According to the myth, what season is it when Persephone is in the underworld? How do you know?

   The season is ________________. I know this because the text says,

   ______________________________________________

   ______________________________________________.

5. What is one question you had about the text as you read? What did you do to find the answer?

   ______________________________________________

   ______________________________________________

NAME ______________________________

# Literature Central Message

Read the passage. Use it to answer the questions on pages 15 and 16.

## How the Raccoon Outwitted the Fox

1 A wise old raccoon sat up in a tree near the river. The raccoon saw the fox play a sly trick on a bear, and he did not like it. This was not the first trick the fox had played.

2 "The fox is getting a big head," said the raccoon. "He thinks he has the cunning of all the animals and that no one can outwit him. Someone must play a 'fox trick' on him."

3 Later, the raccoon saw the fox coming down the trail. The raccoon was eating some juicy yellow apples. As soon as he saw the fox, he ran up a tree and began to smack his lips.

4 The fox stopped under the tree. "What tastes so good?" he asked.

5 For answer, the raccoon threw down an apple to the fox. The fox took the apple and ate it. "Where did you get it?" he asked when he had finished the last mouthful.

6 The raccoon gave the fox directions to a tree filled with juicy yellow apples.

7 "But you can climb the tree and pick your own apples," whined the fox. "How can I get them off the tree?"

8 "Oh, that's easy," said the raccoon. "Just back off two bow shots from the tree. Then, lower your head, run hard, and butt the tree. You have such a big head that it will shake the tree hard enough for all the apples to fall at once."

9 The fox thanked the raccoon and started at once. He found the apple tree, just where the raccoon had said. "I will get such a fine start that when I hit the tree it will shake the world," thought the fox. Already he began, in his mind, to see the apples falling like pine needles and to feel the earth shaking under his feet.

10 The fox closed his eyes, lowered his head, and ran swiftly over the thick grass. He struck the tree as hard as he could with his big head. Not a single apple fell, but a dazed, foolish-looking fox fell to the ground.

11 The next morning as the sun rose, a shame-faced fox was seen running toward the woods. He carried his head low, and he seemed to be playing no foxy tricks. The raccoon, hidden in a tree out of sight, nodded to himself with satisfaction.

NAME ______________________________

# Guided Practice Central Message

**1.** What are the most important events in the story?

In a fable, the moral is often clear because one important event causes another important event to happen. To find a story's moral, start by looking for key events. To decide if an event is key, ask yourself, "Does this action move the story forward?" For example, think about these events from the beginning of the fable: 1) The raccoon sat up in a tree near the river and 2) The raccoon saw the fox play a trick on a bear. Which one is the cause of another important event? Which one is key to the story? It's the second one. The raccoon saw the fox play a trick on a bear, and that caused the raccoon to play a trick on the fox.

If you were going to tell a friend what the fable "How the Raccoon Outwitted the Fox" was about, which events would you need to include? Write a key event from the beginning, the middle, and the end of the story.

Beginning— ______________________________

Middle— ______________________________

End— ______________________________

Does the first key event you chose lead to the second? Does the second lead to the third? If so, there is a good chance you can find a moral based on those key events.

**2.** What happened to the main character at the end of the story, and why?

In a fable, the main character has usually done something to bring about his or her own fate in the end. To find the moral, you need to know what happened to the main character at the end and what that character did to bring about his or her fate.

What happened to the fox at the end of the story? What did the fox do at the beginning of the story that led to this result? Write your answers in complete sentences.

______________________________

______________________________

NAME ________________________________

## Independent Practice Central Message

**1.** Reread paragraph 2, below. The raccoon thinks the fox is too pleased with himself. Underline the text that shows this is what the raccoon thinks.

> 2 "The fox is getting a big head," said the raccoon. "He thinks he has the cunning of all the animals and that no one can outwit him. Someone must play a 'fox trick' on him."

**2.** Reread the final paragraph, below. Underline the text that shows the fox felt embarrassed or ashamed.

> 11 The next morning as the sun rose, a shame-faced fox was seen running toward the woods. He carried his head low, and he seemed to be playing no foxy tricks. The raccoon, hidden in a tree out of sight, nodded to himself with satisfaction.

**3.** Review the final paragraph. How did the raccoon feel at the end of the story? How do you know?

At the end of the story, the raccoon felt ____________________. I know this because the text says, ________________________________________________

________________________________________________________________.

**4.** Look at the title again. Now that you have read the story, what do you think the word *outwitted* means?

*Outwitted* means ________________________________________________.

**5.** The purpose of a fable is to teach a lesson. What lesson or moral can be learned from this fable?

________________________________________________________________

________________________________________________________________

________________________________________________________________

NAME ____________________

# Literature Supporting Details

Read the passage. Use it to answer the questions on pages 18 and 19.

## The Stonecutter

1 One day, a stonecutter worked under the hot sun. He was very unhappy with his life. He hit the rock before him over and over. A wealthy lord passed by in a lovely carriage. The stonecutter watched and felt jealous of the lord's wealth.

2 "There he goes, in his fancy carriage with not a care in the world," said the stonecutter. "If only I could be a man of privilege myself."

3 A moment later, the stonecutter found himself jolting along in a carriage. He was wearing a heavy velvet robe sewn with gold thread. He could not believe his luck! As the carriage went along, though, he grew unhappy. The robe was hot. The carriage bounced uncomfortably. The stonecutter demanded to be let out.

4 As he sat roasting in the sun by the side of the road, he said, "The sun is more powerful than even a wealthy man. It is making me miserable. If only I could be the powerful sun."

5 No sooner had the words left his mouth than the man found himself blazing in the sky. He had become the powerful sun! He shone his golden light on all of the world. Before long, a large, gray cloud came between the sun and a spot where he wanted to shine. No matter how he tried, he could not shine past the cloud.

6 "The sun is not as powerful as I had thought!" he exclaimed. "Clouds are more powerful than even the sun. Oh, I wish that I, too, could be a cloud."

7 Instantly, the man changed into a cloud. With great joy, he created rain and thunder. He threw bolts of lightning at trees and houses. When he tried to blast a rock with lightning, he failed. He tried again, but nothing happened.

8 "The rock is more powerful than a cloud," he thought in surprise. "I wish to be a strong and steady rock." The man got his wish but soon felt himself being chipped away by a chisel. It was a stonecutter at work. The man realized how foolish he had been. Nothing, it seemed, was more powerful than a stonecutter.

9 "Oh, to be myself once again!" the man thought. He found himself with a mallet and chisel in hand, staring at the rock before him. He smiled, positioned his chisel on the rock, and swung his mallet, breaking off a perfect piece of stone. From that moment on, the stonecutter was happy with his life. He never again believed that others held all the power.

NAME ______________________________

## Guided Practice Supporting Details

**1.** How does the stonecutter feel at the beginning of the story?

One lesson you could learn from "The Stonecutter" is *Be content with who you are*. The specific details in the story work together to teach this lesson. Many of the key details relate to how the stonecutter is feeling at a given point in time. His feelings throughout the story lead to the lesson in the end.

Reread paragraph 1, below, and pay special attention to the underlined words.

1 One day, a stonecutter worked under the hot sun. He was very unhappy with his life. <u>He hit the rock before him over and over.</u> A wealthy lord passed by in a lovely carriage. The stonecutter watched and felt jealous of the lord's wealth.

The underlined sentence shows how the stonecutter is feeling about his life. Which adjectives best describe how he's feeling?

**A.** content and at peace  **B.** confused and afraid
**C.** excited and hopeful  **D.** angry and sad

**2.** The stonecutter has very similar feelings each time he is granted a wish (until he becomes the rock). Review the table below. What pattern do you notice? How does this pattern teach us to be happy with who we are?

| What He Has Become | How He Feels at First | How He Feels Later |
|---|---|---|
| a wealthy lord | He could not believe his luck! | If only I could be the powerful sun. |
| the sun | He shone his golden light. | The sun is not as powerful as I thought. |
| a cloud | With great joy, he created rain and thunder. | The rock is more powerful than a cloud. I wish to be a strong and steady rock. |

I noticed ______________________________________________

______________________________________________________.

This teaches us to be happy with who we are by ____________________

NAME ____________________

## Independent Practice Supporting Details

**1.** Reread paragraph 3. Why was the stonecutter unhappy after becoming a wealthy lord? Use specific details from the text in your answer.

______________________________________________

______________________________________________

**2.** Which of these details from the story best supports the idea that even a stonecutter has power?

**A.** The stonecutter smiled and went back to work with his mallet and chisel.

**B.** The stonecutter's wishes for more power were granted one after the other.

**C.** When the man was a rock, only a stonecutter had power over him.

**D.** When he was upset, the stonecutter hit the rock over and over again.

**3.** Reread paragraph 8, below. What do the underlined details show?

> 8 "The rock is more powerful than a cloud," he thought in surprise. "I wish to be a strong and steady rock." The man got his wish but soon felt himself being chipped away by a chisel. It was a stonecutter at work. The man realized how foolish he had been. Nothing, it seemed, was more powerful than a stonecutter.

______________________________________________

______________________________________________

______________________________________________

**4.** Often, a story teaches more than one lesson. Which of the lessons below are supported by the details in "The Stonecutter"? Circle all that apply.

**A.** Nothing in life is important.

**B.** A good attitude makes a good life.

**C.** What others have may not be as great as it seems.

**D.** Find what makes you powerful, and you will be happy.

NAME ______________________

## Literature Character Traits

Read the passage. Use it to answer the questions below and on page 21.

### Prepared to Play

1 Mia sat slumped at the piano bench. She hung her head, and her shoulders curled toward the piano.

2 "Do you want to take a break and try again later?" Mia's mom asked.

3 Mia stiffened and banged the heel of one hand on the piano keys. "No, Mom! I've got it," she replied. Mia wasn't really angry at her mother. She was angry at herself for not having practiced more. Two hours a day wasn't enough. The piano festival was only two days away, and Mia felt completely unprepared.

4 Mia took a deep breath. She tucked one springy lock of brown hair behind her ear and positioned her hands. Mia began to play, but she was rushing through the notes. It wasn't long before her fingers felt tangled.

5 "Arrgh," growled Mia. She wished that she were sick or had broken a finger so she wouldn't have to play in the festival. But then, she thought of her grandma. Nana had loved to play. When she played piano, her hands flowed over the keys and a look of contentment filled her face.

6 Mia sat up and whispered, "You can do this." Once more, she began to play. A smile spread across her face as her fingers moved effortlessly from key to key.

## Guided Practice Character Traits

1. Characters express their feelings in different ways. Reread the first paragraph. How does Mia show that she feels discouraged?

______________________________________________

______________________________________________

2. How a character thinks of himself or herself can be a trait, too. Reread the third paragraph. Underline the details that show Mia might be too hard on herself.

3. The author tells us only one thing about Mia's physical appearance. What is it?

______________________________________________

______________________________________________

NAME ______________________

## Independent Practice Character Traits

**1.** Name a character trait that describes Mia's mother. Explain your answer.

______________________

______________________

**2.** Reread paragraph 3. How did Mia show her anger?

______________________

______________________

**3.** Reread paragraph 5. What helped Mia overcome her negative feelings?

______________________

______________________

**4.** Look at the following details from the text.

- Mia practiced piano for two hours every day.
- Mia was upset with how she was playing, but she did not quit.
- Mia told herself she could do it and played once more.

Which character trait do these details most clearly support?

**A.** lazy **B.** caring
**C.** determined **D.** grumpy

**5.** Reread paragraph 6 below.

> 6 Mia sat up and whispered, "You can do this." Once more, she began to play. A smile spread across her face as her fingers moved effortlessly from key to key.

What does the underlined sentence show about Mia's personality?

**A.** Mia does not believe in herself.
**B.** Mia does not like trying new things.
**C.** Mia likes to pretend that she is her grandma.
**D.** Mia knows how to get her feelings under control.

NAME ____________________

# Literature Character Feelings and Actions

Read the passage. Use it to answer the questions on pages 23 and 24.

## Speaking Up

1 Carlos sat glumly at the kitchen table. He had made himself a snack, but he didn't feel very hungry.

2 "Hey, Carlos," said Rosa, slamming the door. She plopped her books down and helped herself to a slice of his apple.

3 "What's going on?" Rosa asked. "You look kind of down."

4 Carlos sighed. "Do you remember my friend Micah?" Rosa nodded. "Well, some kids have been giving him a hard time. They've been teasing him about being short, and about wearing glasses. I hate the way they're treating him. He tries to act like it doesn't bother him, but I know it does."

5 Rosa shook her head. "That's awful! You know those kids are bullies, right?"

6 Carlos nodded. "I tried to stick up for him a couple of times," he said, "but no one really listened to me." He slumped down in his chair.

7 "Listen," said Rosa, scooting closer to Carlos, "we're going to make a plan. The first thing is for you to tell a teacher. Do you feel like you can talk to Ms. D'Angelo about it?"

8 "She's a good listener," Carlos said. "I could probably tell her."

9 "Okay, that's a good start," replied Rosa. "Now, this is hard to do, but you could also speak up the next time those kids bother Micah. You don't have to be mean, but you can tell them you don't like what they're doing."

10 Carlos took a deep breath. "But what if they still don't listen?" he asked.

11 Rosa took a bite of apple and thought for a moment. "Do you think there are any other kids who have also been afraid to speak up?" she asked.

12 "Yeah," said Carlos. "I know Cameron and Molly don't like what's been happening. Kenji, Sam, and Alyssa would be on our side, too," he added.

13 "Perfect!" said Rosa. "The more allies you have, the better. As a group, you can let the other kids know that the way they're treating Micah isn't cool."

14 Carlos looked relieved. "Thanks, Rosa," he said, giving his sister a hug. "I feel better now that I have a plan. I'm going to go call Micah and tell him about it," he said, pushing back his chair and standing up.

NAME ____________________

# Guided Practice Character Feelings and Actions

Often, how the main character feels drives the action in a story. For example, if the main character has a problem and is upset about it, the story will very likely be about trying to fix that problem. That's how the story "Speaking Up" is set up. To figure out the main problem, pay close attention to the main character's actions and feelings.

1. Reread paragraphs 1 through 3 of "Speaking Up." Which character is upset? Use details from the text to explain how you know.

______________________________________________

______________________________________________

How characters act together gives us clues about their relationship. Throughout the story, Rosa does things that show she and Carlos are close. This makes it believable that the two are brother and sister.

2. How does Rosa act like a sister? Before we are told that Rosa is Carlos's sister, we are given a few clues that suggest a close relationship. Reread paragraph 2, below. Underline the words in the paragraph that give the biggest clue that Rosa is Carlos's sister. Then, explain how the underlined words serve as a clue.

2 "Hey, Carlos," said Rosa, slamming the door. She plopped her books down and helped herself to a slice of his apple.

______________________________________________

______________________________________________

3. Review the first three paragraphs. Pay attention to Carlos's actions and Rosa's words. How does Rosa know something is wrong with Carlos before he says anything?

______________________________________________

______________________________________________

NAME ______________________

## Independent Practice Character Feelings and Actions

1. Which sibling do you think is older, Carlos or Rosa? Explain your answer with evidence from the story.

______________________

______________________

______________________

2. Like most stories, "Speaking Up" is driven by a problem. What problem is Carlos having?

______________________

______________________

______________________

3. Which of these quotations shows why Carlos wants to help Micah?
   - **A.** "I hate the way they're treating him" (paragraph 4).
   - **B.** "I tried to stick up for him a couple of times" (paragraph 6).
   - **C.** "She's a good listener" (paragraph 8).
   - **D.** "But what if they still don't listen?" (paragraph 10).

4. Which of these actions makes it clear that Carlos felt much better after talking to Rosa?
   - **A.** He told Rosa about his friend Micah's problem.
   - **B.** He listed some kids who might help Micah.
   - **C.** He pushed back his chair and stood up.
   - **D.** He looked relieved.

5. After he calls Micah, what action do you predict Carlos will take? Explain why you think this will happen.

______________________

______________________

NAME ______________________________

## Performance Task

Read the texts. Use them to complete each step in the task that follows.

### The Fox and the Goat

1 A Fox fell into a well and could not get out again. After some time, a thirsty Goat came by and asked if the water was good.

2 "The finest in the whole country," said the crafty Fox. "Jump in and try it." The Goat jumped in and began to drink. The Fox quickly jumped on the Goat's back and leaped out of the well.

3 The foolish Goat begged the Fox to help him out, but the Fox was already on his way to the woods.

4 "If you had as much sense as you have beard," he said, "you would have been more cautious about finding a way out before you jumped in."

5 Moral: *Look before you leap.*

### The Fox and the Stork

1 "Come dine with me today," the Fox said to the Stork one day. For dinner, the Fox served soup in a very shallow dish. All the Stork could do was to wet the very tip of his long bill. The Fox lapped it up easily.

2 The Stork was displeased. He invited the Fox to dine with him and made a lovely fish dinner. It was served in a tall jar with a narrow neck. The Stork could easily reach the food with his long bill, but the Fox could only lick the outside of the jar. The Fox left in a huff, angry at the trick the Stork had played.

3 Moral: *Do not play tricks on your neighbors unless you can stand the same treatment yourself.*

### The Rooster and the Fox

1 One evening, Fox trotted up to a tree where wise Rooster rested. "Have you heard the wonderful news?" cried the Fox.

2 "What news?" asked the Rooster.

3 "Your family and mine and all other animals have agreed to live in peace and friendship. Do come down, and let us celebrate."

4 "How wonderful!" said the Rooster. He stretched up on tiptoes.

5 "What is it you see?" asked the Fox.

6 "It looks like a couple of Dogs coming this way." The Fox immediately began to run off.

7 "Wait," cried the Rooster. "Why do you run? The Dogs are friends of yours now!"

8 "They might not have heard the news," answered the Fox.

9 The Rooster smiled, for he had succeeded in outwitting a crafty enemy.

10 Moral: *The trickster is easily tricked.*

NAME ______________________________

## Performance Task

1. Ask a question about "The Rooster and the Fox" that will help you understand how the Fox is the Rooster's enemy.

______________________________

______________________________

2. Answer the question you wrote above. If the answer cannot be found in the text, take your best guess based on the details in the text.

______________________________

______________________________

______________________________

3. Which cause-and-effect relationship is most clearly shown in "The Fox and the Stork"?

   **A.** The Fox was kind to the Stork, so the Stork was kind to the Fox.

   **B.** The Stork was kind to the Fox, so the Fox was kind to the Stork.

   **C.** The Fox was mean to the Stork, so the Stork was mean to the Fox.

   **D.** The Stork was mean to the Fox, so the Fox was mean to the Stork.

4. The moral of "The Fox and the Goat" is *Look before you leap.* Which two key events work best together to teach this moral?

______________________________

______________________________

______________________________

______________________________

______________________________

______________________________

NAME ____________________

## Performance Task

**5.** Which of the morals below could apply to each of the three fables?

**A.** Be kind to others.
**B.** Everyone likes a good joke.
**C.** Don't trust a trickster.
**D.** Money does not buy happiness.

**6.** In "The Rooster and the Fox," the Rooster believes that all the animals had agreed to live in peace. Circle one.

True False

**7.** Plan a fable that teaches young children to share their toys. Imagine the fable will be turned into a play and acted out for a group of preschoolers. In order to make your lesson clear, something must happen in the beginning of the story that causes something else to happen in the middle, which leads to something even more important happening in the end. Your characters need to have very clear personality traits, which they show through their actions, not just their words.

Use the graphic organizer on page 28 to plan your fable. Then, use the rubric below to evaluate your story plan. For each topic, circle *Proficient*, *Learning*, or *Beginner*. This will help you know what skills you need to work on.

| | **Proficient** | **Learning** | **Beginner** |
|---|---|---|---|
| **Key Events** | Key events in the beginning, middle, and end show a clear cause-and-effect relationship. | Key events in the beginning, middle, and end show a somewhat clear cause-and-effect relationship. | Key events in the beginning, middle, and end do not clearly show a cause-and-effect relationship. |
| **Moral** | The moral is strongly supported by the key events. | The moral is somewhat supported by the key events. | The moral is hardly supported by the key events. |
| **Character Actions** | The characters' actions are specific and clear so that preschoolers can understand what is happening. | The characters' actions are not very specific or clear, making it difficult for a preschooler to understand what is happening. | The character's actions are not clearly described, making it very hard for a preschooler to understand what is happening. |
| **Character Traits** | Each character's traits match the actions the character takes. | One character's traits match the actions that character takes. | The characters' traits do not clearly match their actions. |

NAME ______________________________

**Performance Task**

# Fable Graphic Organizer

## Characters and Their Traits

Character 1 ______________________
______________________
______________________
______________________

Character 2 ______________________
______________________
______________________
______________________

### Action in the Beginning

______________________

### Action in the Middle

______________________

### Action in the End

______________________

## Moral

______________________
______________________

NAME ____________________

## Assessment

Read the passage. Use evidence from the text to answer the questions that follow.

### Tia's Turtle

1 "Grab some paints," Mr. Green told the class. "Remember to sketch your portion of the mural in pencil first." The students milled around. They chose places to sit and talked to each other about what they planned to paint.

2 Akeelah raised her hand. "Can we use pictures from our books for ideas?" she asked.

3 Mr. Green nodded. "Sure, I just don't want you to copy whole scenes. Show me your own creative underwater scenes."

4 Tia, Jake, and Emma found a spot and settled down to work. "What are you going to start with, Tia?" asked Emma, beginning a coral reef.

5 "A sea turtle," replied Tia, flipping through an animal encyclopedia. She loved the giant turtles. In a video, the class had seen a mother nesting on the beach. When the eggs hatched, the tiny turtles crawled over the sand to reach the ocean.

6 "Your coral looks great, Emma!" Jake exclaimed. "You're both such good artists," he added. "Whatever I come up with is probably going to wreck the mural." He shook his head and erased the two marks he'd made.

7 "Come on, Jake," said Tia. "Just start with something simple, like a fish."

8 The three friends worked quietly, each focused on his or her own drawing. Tia took out a bottle of green paint and began to fill in her turtle's outline.

9 "Check this out!" said Emma excitedly. Tia was startled and turned quickly. Her hand knocked over the paint. It tipped and a puddle of green spread across the mural. Tia's cheeks burned. She covered her face and tried not to cry. She could feel a hand patting her back. Tia peeked between her fingers. Akeelah was standing beside her. Emma was sopping up the green paint. Jake grinned. "Thank goodness you covered up my fish!" he said. "It was totally lousy."

10 "It's no big deal," Emma agreed. "My coral looked way too small. We can use the green paint that spilled to make a giant turtle this time."

11 Tia heaved a sigh. "Thanks, you guys. I'm sorry I messed up everyone's—"

12 "Seriously," Jake interrupted. "You saved the day."

13 Tia laughed as she picked up her paintbrush and got to work on her new supersized turtle.

NAME ____________________

## Assessment

**Part 1: I can ask and answer questions about literature.**

**1.** Write two questions about the story "Tia's Turtle." Include one question that helps deepen your understanding of what you read.

______________________________

______________________________

**2.** Answer one of your questions from item 1. If the answer cannot be found in the text, take your best guess based on the details in the text.

______________________________

______________________________

**3.** Skim the story for the word *mural.* Avoiding the question "What does *mural* mean?" what could you ask to figure out the meaning?

______________________________

**4.** What was the subject of the mural Mr. Green had assigned to his class?

**A.** sea turtles
**B.** a coral reef
**C.** underwater life
**D.** rainforest animals

**5.** Underline the sentence below that shows the main problem in the story.

> 9 "Check this out!" said Emma excitedly. Tia was startled and turned quickly. Her hand knocked over the paint. It tipped and a puddle of green spread across the mural. Tia's cheeks burned. She covered her face and tried not to cry...

**Part 2: I can determine the central message of a literary text and find key details that support it.**

**1.** How did Tia's friends react when she spilled the paint? Use specific details from the text in your answer.

______________________________

NAME ____________________

## Assessment

2. How do the friends feel at the end of the story?

   **A.** angry
   **B.** cheerful
   **C.** proud
   **D.** sad

3. Reread paragraph 5, below. How does the underlined sentence relate to the story's ending?

   > 5 "A sea turtle," replied Tia, flipping through an animal encyclopedia. She loved the giant turtles. In a video, the class had seen a mother nesting on the beach. When the eggs hatched, the tiny turtles crawled over the sand to reach the ocean.

   ________________________________________

   ________________________________________

4. Which sentence best expresses the central message of the story?

   **A.** Everyone has different talents.
   **B.** Friends are always making silly mistakes.
   **C.** It's always best to listen to your teacher.
   **D.** Good friends care about each other's feelings.

5. Which detail from the story best supports the central message?

   **A.** Emma and Jake made Tia feel better about spilling the paint.
   **B.** Mr. Green wanted the students to paint their own creative scenes.
   **C.** Jake thought he was going to ruin the mural with what he painted.
   **D.** Tia felt so bad about spilling the paint that she almost started to cry.

6. Describe in your own words another key event from the story that supports the central message. Write your answer in complete sentences.

   ________________________________________

   ________________________________________

   ________________________________________

NAME ____________________

## Assessment

**Part 3: I can describe a character's traits, motivations, feelings, and actions.**

1. Match the character with the action. Write the correct letter on the line.

| | |
|---|---|
| ____ Akeelah | **A.** encouraged Jake to start painting |
| ____ Tia | **B.** complimented his/her friends' work |
| ____ Jake | **C.** patted Tia's back to make her feel better |

2. Which words and phrases describe Jake as a character? Circle all that apply.

| | | | |
|---|---|---|---|
| afraid of fish | easygoing | forgetful | funny |
| kind | not confident | rude | too serious |

3. Which sentence from the text most clearly shows that Jake did not think he was a good artist?

_______________________________________________

4. Which detail from the text shows that Tia was really upset?
   - **A.** Tia's cheeks burned (paragraph 9).
   - **B.** Tia peeked between her fingers (paragraph 9).
   - **C.** Tia could feel a hand patting her back (paragraph 9).

5. Reread paragraph 10, below. Which of Emma's character traits does the paragraph show?

> 10 "It's no big deal," Emma agreed. "My coral looked way too small. We can use the green paint that spilled to make a giant turtle this time."

   - **A.** shy and afraid
   - **B.** jealous and selfish
   - **C.** caring and easygoing
   - **D.** talented and confident

6. Reread paragraph 11, below. What does this detail show about how Tia felt?

> 11 Tia heaved a sigh. "Thanks, you guys. I'm sorry I messed up everyone's—"

_______________________________________________

# Answer Key

## Page 9

**1.** Answers will vary but may include: Who is Mr. Wylon? Who is Jackson? What will Jackson miss if he walks away? What does Mr. Wylon mean when he says, "Let's get a move on!"? **2.** Answers will vary but may include: What happened to the cat-food bowl? When did Akito adopt the cat? Where was the cat-food bowl left? How long was the bowl left out? **3.** Answers will vary but may include: How did Jackson know the visitor was not the stray cat? Why was it so hard for Jackson to drag himself away from the window?

## Page 10

**1.** Answers will vary but may include: What kind of animal is eating my pet food? Where did it come from? **2.** Answers will vary but may include: What does *elsewhere* mean? What was Jackson thinking about? **3.** Answers will vary but may include: What do you think the food in the center of the sheet is for? What will happen to the ground if Mr. Wylon and Jackson spray water on it? **4.** Answers will vary but may include: What action would go along with jumping out of bed? How was Jackson feeling at that moment? **5.** Answers will vary. **6.** Answers will vary.

## Page 12

**1.** D; **2.** Demeter loved <u>her daughter/ Persephone</u> more than anything. **3.** A

## Page 13

**1.** A; **2.** Answers will vary but may include: Demeter was angry with Zeus, and she went into mourning for her daughter. **3.** Answers will vary but may include: *He knew that the people would starve if Demeter did not tend the earth as she had always done.* **4.** The season is winter. I know this because the text says *Plants and flowers died, and the world became cold, dark, and dreary.* **5.** Answers will vary.

## Page 15

**1.** Answers will vary but may include: Beginning—The fox played a trick on the bear; Middle—The raccoon told the fox how to get apples from the tree; End—The fox head-butts the tree and is knocked to the ground. **2.** Answers will vary but may include: At the end, the fox hurt his head on the tree and looked foolish. At the beginning, the fox tricked a bear.

# Answer Key

**Page 16**

**1.** Student should underline *"The fox is getting a big head," said the raccoon* and/or *"He thinks he has the cunning of all the animals and that no one can outwit him."* **2.** Student should underline *shame-faced fox, carried his head low,* and *seemed to be playing no foxy tricks.* **3.** Answers will vary but may include: At the end of the story, the raccoon felt pleased/satisfied. I know this because the text says *The raccoon...nodded to himself with satisfaction.* **4.** *Outwitted* means to defeat or trick someone by being more clever.
**5.** Answers will vary but may include: Be careful what you do to others because it may be done to you.

**Page 18**

**1.** D; **2.** Answers will vary but may include: I noticed that each time, he is happy at first, but then he wants to become something more powerful. He is never satisfied with what he has, no matter how good it is. This teaches us to be happy with who we are by showing that being someone or something else does not make us happy.

**Page 19**

**1.** Answers will vary but may include: His robe was hot, and the carriage ride was bumpy. **2.** C; **3.** Answers will vary but may include: These details show that the stonecutter is more powerful than the rock, which had seemed like the most powerful thing just a moment before. They also show that by wishing to be more powerful, the man got himself into a worse situation. **4.** Choices B, C, and D are all supported by the story's details.

**Page 20**

**1.** Mia slumped and hung her head, and her shoulders curled toward the piano. **2.** Student should underline *She was angry at herself for not having practiced more. Two hours a day wasn't enough.* **3.** Mia has brown, curly hair.

**Page 21**

**1.** Answers will vary but may include: Caring—She knows Mia is frustrated and suggests that she take a break. **2.** She stiffened, banged her hand on the keys, and yelled at her mother. **3.** She thought about her grandma playing the piano. **4.** C; **5.** D

# Answer Key

## Page 23

**1.** Answers will vary but may include: Carlos is upset. I know because he sat glumly at the table and he didn't feel hungry. **2.** Answers will vary but may include: The phrase *helped herself to a slice of his apple* shows that Rosa is very comfortable around Carlos. She is probably a close friend or family member. **3.** Answers will vary but may include: Rosa knows Carlos is upset because he looks *kind of down* (paragraph 3). She probably noticed that he was sitting glumly. He might also have had a sad expression on his face.

## Page 24

**1.** Answers will vary but may include: Rosa seems older because she wants to take care of Carlos's problem and because she has lots of good advice. **2.** Carlos's friend is being bullied, and Carlos doesn't know how to help him. **3.** A; **4.** D; **5.** Answers will vary but may include: Carlos will probably talk to the kids he wants to help him stand up to the bullies.

## Performance Task

**1.** Answers will vary but may include: Why did the Fox want the Rooster to come down and celebrate with him? **2.** Answers will vary but may include: The Fox told the Rooster to come down and celebrate with him because he wanted to eat the Rooster. **3.** C; **4.** Answers will vary but may include: The goat wanted to try the water, so he jumped into the well without thinking. **5.** C; **6.** False; **7.** Students should complete the rubric to determine their level of proficiency.

## Assessment

**Part 1: 1.** Answers will vary. **2.** Answers will vary. **3.** Answers will vary but may include: What kind of painting can be broken up into large sections or portions? **4.** C; **5.** Students should underline either *Her hand knocked over the paint* or *It tipped and a puddle of green spread across the mural.*

# Answer Key

**Part 2: 1.** Answers will vary but may include: Akeelah patted her back, Emma cleaned up the paint, and Jake joked that it was good that she had covered up his fish. **2.** B; **3.** Answers will vary but may include: At the end, Emma suggests they fix the painting by turning it into a giant turtle. **4.** D; **5.** A; **6.** Answers will vary but may include: Tia tried to make Jake feel better about his drawing skills; Jake told Emma and Tia they were good artists.

**Part 3: 1.** C, A, B; **2.** Students should circle *easygoing, funny, kind,* and *not confident.* **3.** *Whatever I come up with is probably going to wreck this mural* (paragraph 6). **4.** A; **5.** C; **6.** Answers will vary but may include: It shows Tia felt relieved and grateful for the way her friends reacted but still sorry for what she had done.